CROSSING
THE STREET
TO *PARADIS*

Also by Myra Shapiro

I'll See You Thursday
[poems]

Four Sublets: Becoming a Poet in New York
[memoir]

In Greenwich Village We Talk of Love
[chapbook]

12 Floors Above the Earth
[poems]

When the World Walks Toward You
[poems]

CROSSING
THE STREET
TO *PARADIS*

MYRA
SHAPIRO

KINCHAFOONEE
CREEK PRESS ∞ ATHENS, GA

Book design by Norman Minnick
Cover photo and author photo by Ian Moran

ISBN: 979-8-218-68044-2

Kinchafoonee Creek Press
585 White Circle #29
Athens, Georgia 30605

www.kcpress.org

In dedication to
The Great Mother and The New Father
Community

Contents

I.

II.

III.

VI.

I.

Ginger Tea with John Donne

Death thou shalt die. Quietly I sip,
And suck on the ginger, inviting
The heat of boiled water
To kill the new virus. It lurks
Like TB before we could fight it.
From the start I aimed to be
The one egg ready to meet my match,
Making it say my name. Words
Lay in wait. My grandson
Wants to tattoo those that flew
From my mouth toward my future
In-laws—I barely understood—
I must have poetry in my life—
Spending all our wedding money for
A three-day honeymoon in Nassau.

So many clues to lead me
To the animal I am; these nights
I take hold of the edge of the sheet,
Clutch the hem along my pillow.
I should have known I had claws
Pulling at words for the page
Pulling up poems to be read—
Vying with death's desire to be fed.

Violence and Wonder

Fixated on doubles, hearing *copse*,
thinking trees and death, I'm home
free with the word *fit;* its twoness
within me from birth, a sister's death

at my heels, so I slumped, then stamped
my way forward by throwing
fits. It's a wonder there were those
who would hold me.

Sheltered in bed I took sick, found
myself turning pages. I learned not to die.
Bed. Book. School. Door.
Come close I could hear, keeping a distance.

Marriage, children—How Did I?
Book. School. Door. Go
from Tennessee to
New York City!

Where if I jay-walk,
I fit. And if I sit on a bench
in a copse of trees, pigeons
nod yes.

Words Arrive from Childhood

Once I simply took them in, ate
borscht or *fricassee*
without exceptional pleasure,
ignorant of the day I'd want
to recreate their joy on my tongue,
calling long distance—my sister—
to ask how many cups of cottage cheese
in Mama's *lokshen kugel.*

Today I baked it for a friend;
she's lost her mate, and at the funeral
an old man I hadn't seen in years
greeted me with my father's
vaudeville corn—*Hello the other day!*

Instantly it took me
to the cockamamie
magic of its meaning.

Curls and Bangs

Don't you dare cut my hair!

When people ask my Russian mother
in her crown of black braids
where my blonde curls come from,
she laughs, "Must be Pushkin."

I talk to my doll. Her name is
Gloria. Her hair is golden, no curls.
Bangs cover her forehead.
My crayon makes an L under them

and an O around her belly button
and a VE below so she knows
she's mine. My word says
she won't get sick, or mad,

or have to fight her way on
to a swing. No one knows
I can spell. No picture sees
I can smile.

We move to a little town
down south; we have a house
on Dug Gap Road. Here
is no playground. Here is

very slow, they don't yell.
No one speaks Yiddish.
Everyone speaks English
but not the way I do.

Betty Ann lives next door—
she's in third grade like me—
we can play in her yard. When
her mother comes out, her hands

run through my hair.
"Where are your horns?"
she asks. I must ask my mother.

Said

In the book of Genesis
In the part that goes "He said
'Let there be light
And there was light'"
I'm suddenly aware of
Light separate from darkness
    Said
        into being.

           And when
In the middle of 6th grade
I came home
In the middle of the day

          Blood
     I said
Blood on my underpants
Mama slapped me!

Her mother had done the same
        She said
That was the way
A girl becomes a woman.

On Finding My 1945 Diary

It is autumn
in Dalton, Georgia.

One line one month ago
World War II ended.

I am going to the movies
with my friend

to moon over
Dana Andrews.

I note, for Eternity,
he doesn't kiss like Billy.

Bastrop

Bastrop. You're not yet wed
To words; you are
17 years old, a freshman
Invited by the best dancer

To Bastrop, a town of parks
Not far from Texas U.,
With him and another couple
For the night, and

You don't turn to say
What a weird word, Bastrop.
You want to go with him,
Cook out together,

You don't know the other
Couple will go into a room
Alone, you don't know she won't return
Leaving you to room with

Him—this is 1949—you only go so far—
It's understood—3rd base—
Suddenly he's Home. Your marriage
Bastrop-born. 70 years later

Bastrop pops up in your head
Why? you wonder—the word
Your story, only he's not
Alive, your husband, the man

Who acts, no questions asked,
(Scorpio to your Gemini)
And you'll lie in the plot
Next to him. Bastrop.

II.

This Is a Photograph of Us

Newly married
Confident as models
On a runway—at 23 I stride
Beside my husband
On the way to *Guys and Dolls*—
His first time in New York City—
His tie waving in the wind,
My high-heeled pumps
Securely fastened—each step
Ensuring encores!

The Knowledge I Have Everything
in the Garden

At 10:30 last night, on 1st Avenue,
a man in a black jacket
a tall man with a mustache
was picking out a cantaloupe.

O New York! You give me
63° and a whole moon
in November, pyramids of fruit
stacked up on the sidewalk

and my friend, I'm walking with
my arm around my friend,
coming from a play
that had 11 women talking with

a love for household lamps,
snakehandling, plastics
as an image of eternity, and, right here,
on your east side

a handsome man giving his nose
to the sweetness of a melon.

Put the Kettle On

Tea? I've begun to ask each evening
partway between dinner and bedtime,
and he's begun to answer *Yes.*

It's an old marriage. We're beginning
to merge. Just this month, arms aching,
I began following his morning routine,
a hot shower so my arms move
with ease. In his case it's knees.

Last night I wanted to sit next to him
as he sat on the side of the bed, simply
to chat a bit about the Middle East,
the peace talks he's been listening to—
and what else was important today?

I wanted to hear his excitement before we go
to our separate sides of the bed,
our particular pillows   and the good sleep.
It's all just begun, the new year. March
is here, and we're living it.

Slap and Eat

And Live. We breathe
delivered by the doctor
with a slap to the behind,
then drink, calmed by milk
from mother's breast.
                              Walking
to a restaurant today, I see a woman
talking to a stroller without a baby
in it; she turns around to me
and says "You're old!"
                              A slap
before I eat, struck
as I was 90 years ago.
Now comfort comes with cappuccino.

*

War between Israelis and Palestinians
led to an Accord when they sat down
                              to eat.
Oslo it was called because Norwegians urged
"Let's eat together." My husband, in alliance,
beside himself with joy, wanted food
to celebrate so we went to eat
and raised a glass
                              L'Chaim!

To life. Fulfilled by food, someday
we'll feed the worms. *L'Chaim!*

These Are the Pearls

It's *Besame Mucho* coming through
revolving doors. It's 2018, the future
far from songs we danced to
left inside me. A waiter stands
to take my order.
                    O waiter,
bring me fresh plums on a plate.

He'd refuse to eat. Patiently,
his caretaker urged, "We want you
to be well; if you won't eat, she'll kill me."
He smiled, "Then we'll have to go to your funeral."
He could do that—Southern charmer
to the end.

To find him open the kitchen cabinet:
Coca-Cola, a bag of Cheetos,
the salt inside the shaker he would fill;
a half jar of Skippy peanut butter
still intact. I don't want it.
                    It's more than I can fathom!—
the whole of the kitchen. The future
filled with *Besame Mucho* and blintzes
he stored in the freezer.

Thaw little pancakes...
Flicker flicker...
I am speaking of his flashlights in the drawer.

The Arc of Your Foot on My Foot

Two animals we were—you entering
me as if that was what
I was there for
               the flood
of you pouring
into me. When a dove came
announcing new life, we made
                         home
vowing I do and You do,
creating arms and legs
and eyes and hearts we called
                        family—
Listen to the warmth! Entwined
and sometimes difficult
to breathe we hung together until
                        gravity
pulled us apart
no longer the Arc
of your Foot on my Foot
                  my body
                  filling the air

after The Couple *by Louise Bourgeois*

Here I Am

Out of an ecocardiogram on York—
the 57th St. bus on the corner
waiting—spur of a moment
I climb on—a boy gives me his seat—
and, urban to the core, I'm in

my world—past Lexington
to 5th where I decide to exit—
lit up possibilities along the way
to 53rd to MOMA
to The Modern, where

waiting hands will feed me
while words from other worlds
surround me as I eat, with gusto,
each buttered bread crumb,
cod with endive, mushrooms, pesto

before I catch a movie
two escalators below
the waiter leads me to, attentive
to the cane I hold, and there, waiting,
a theater fills up   row by row

here we are!   privileged
to see a rerun of a Buñuel film, alive
to *The Exterminating Angel.*

Comrades

Reading a poem about reaching

In pity, offering a hankie, the poet

Olds to the writer Hardwick,

Whose nose drips during her talk

About Lowell's offering

A cherry branch to Pasternak's grave,

I remember mid-January 1991, there

The month the USSR falls, and I am

Reciting for my fellow travelers

Tsvetaeva's words

    all of us will
        sleep under the earth, we who
        never let each other sleep above it.

III.

Going Viral

We kept saying it, the word
viral, excited by a tweet
that went that way. The word
sounding out its loud *I*
grew ordinary,
without mystery.
We didn't hear doom
when ordering
avocado toast, saying
it was *going viral*—
until

it upped the ante
on every continent, even out
to sea. Royally it spoke:
You will reverence me
in your history books. Beyond
millennials. The elderly
will testify to my entrance
on Broadway, a crown
upon my head, *Coronavirus*—
striding the red carpet,
piling up the syllables.

Locked-Down / Sweeping Up

"And when Peace here does house
He comes with work to do, he does not come to coo"

—Gerard Manley Hopkins

Sweeping up words,
marking time: March
April May turning to song

I ain't had no lovin' since
January, February, June or July—

releasing dreams, words
the warmth I wake from:

swimming to an island
with a suitcase in my hand, I land
where others gather, looking up
a recipe for peas: Take a glass bowl,
with your palm help the peas stay
inside, not float away. Mother
is the cook, but

not of locked down peas.
She loved the slots, cherries
twirling together
to the sway of her arm.
I don't want to have her
welcome me where she lives
westward toward a pair o' dice.

they're putting me away

or I am putting me away
       and you who'll walk in
where we slept   to love to dream
while on the wall hung
heightened moments from my life

you who'll come to take this place
         or look it over
will not know

what's nailed once flew
to New York City
from Tennessee, Canada and France

      the boat with no one in it
      on an empty river
      gave up Chattanooga

      the watercolored animal—an ass—
      two men's heads emerging
      from its back, its ears up
      to catch their conversation
      made us laugh in Banff

      the goldfish jumping
      high above the ocean's waves
      entered through a poem by Mark Doty
      we'd brought to a friend who invited us
      to share last days in Paris

And so they came
to hang with us

Full

Blueberries are content to fill the bowl.

Roses from the roof fill up a vase.

Hours loom. I'll try to fill this page.

Words lock down inside a quilt.

My bed says lay my head upon.

It is noon. July 22nd 2021.

There is lunch and there is dinner.

There is my family alive on Zoom.

There is nothing more to say.

Erase line 5. Then get a sonnet.

Push. Pretend you're giving birth.

Push harder. Become a comet.

There is kinship and there is mirth.

There is Yiddish, my mother's laughter.

Make her *kugel,* bake *rugalach* for after.

S O S

I had no heat.
I had no internet
Nor anyone to proposition
In my bed.

Dreams had fled. Out the window
Cranes swayed, building what
Comes next. I can try to
Fix the internet

I can call for help
To get the heat.
I can bundle up and eat.
I want

To put words
On a page, lines that lead to
Eager prepositions.

Heat

Broken boiler
Distancing me from home,
I'm at my daughter's apartment
With seven poets on Zoom
Meant to keep us
In the warmth of poems,
But where are the fires
Of yesteryear?

In the rain, in the cold
I go out to 7th Ave, unknown
Neighborhood, toward a sign
On the corner   CAFETERIA
Where a man stands at the door—
He'll poach my eggs,
He'll toast my avocado.
My life was meant for this!

Simple

She put on shoes—he put on shoes
She to walk her dogs—he for a Museum
They both came home—many years/cities apart—
And died.

She was my friend's friend, gone
This very week. Her coat still on.

He was my father, come back home,
My mother said, to rest—

Why do I tell you this? Just now

I put on shoes. I left
The house even though
It's cold, even though I'm old
To live my life. Ate lunch:
Cappuccino   a sandwich
A window table.

Over two years of living a
Pandemic, five years since my husband
Died. In the ICU
His friend arrived to remind him—
Get up, we've gotta go to Atlantic City—
That's when he died   smiling

And I wonder if life lived
Leapt to
In one elevated moment
Grounds you—
Something simple
A joke, a swing,
        a thing with feathers

At My Mentor's Memorial

10/22/22

Reading my poem "Family Jokes"
At a mike sung into by
A woman who soon has Covid
I am positive it leaped
Into me. Of course Robert Bly
Started it, the grain of
Wit he insisted on, before
He *agreed to be born.*

IV.

Muscle Shoals

At the Tennessee River in Alabama
A woman sings under the flow.
Natives canoeing her currents
Called the place Muscle Shoals.

Our relatives take us touring; we see
A nondescript shed—The Rolling Stones
Came to it, here Aretha recorded *Respect*.
It's in the middle of nowhere, yet

It's worked its way under our skin:
Soul and beat, black and white,
A force now controlled by a dam.

We take a bridge to Tuscumbia
Where Helen Keller was born
Feral child, blind, deaf and mute,
Her first word *water* from a well.

I may sound like a tour guide
Afraid of mythic depth,
Yet I feel creation surface
Beyond an unknown edge.

At the house our nephew built
With the River up to its side
Deep waves fetch—we hear them—
As we raise our glasses to health—

With history and family
We're passing New Years Eve—
To the decade   my 9th   out to get me
                              where   when

33

Passover 2020

Imagine Moses
leading the slaves
out of Egypt on Zoom.
That's where we are
crossing the Sea of Reeds
to an unknown land

at a Seder on a computer,
trying to capture
not one but ten plagues,
the past as present.
Stories work that way.
We eat the symbols:

bitter herbs for hardship,
salt water for tears,
unleavened bread/matzos,
apples mixed with wine—
Far apart we eat, we sing
for times past, and to come.

My grandson who's autistic
speaks up—surprises us
to announce he feels *privileged*—
his word—which leads me
to ask, "Who in the story
has privilege?"

"Moses," he says immediately.
Straight to our hearts,
a light, it dawns on us:
Moses struggles,
slow of speech, he stutters,
yet he guides, he has visions

he pursues, out of which
words rise for one, two, three religions
alive to this day we've made new.

After

"I have more puzzles to solve."

—David Sharif

My grandson's gone.

David. Named for my father
so he would remain and

yes you within his name
would hold his spirit

David—
avid   avid   David

you wrote a book of poems
The Empowerment of My Condition

carrying on your great grand-father's
passion to take hold

of the world—
the U.S. by trailer—

and you   going global
were seized
                Epilepsy

as I sat writing "After
Doing Crosswords with My Grandson."

This Day in October 2022

the medical examiner's report
—*plunk*—thrown
to the concrete on Yom Kippur

before we return to the synagogue
for the final hours of these Days of Awe
to chant the recitation of forgiving sins and
mourning. A long service. *And it is written
who will live and who will die.*

David by our side last year saying it.
Rabbi Bernstein says, "Stand if you are able."

Gathering Stones

Robert Frost's "Nothing Gold Can Stay"
I read at your grave with Naomi Shihab Nye's
"People do not pass away
They die / And then they stay."

Avid David, your stone is etched
Autism Advocate—World Traveler
Life threw me a curve ball, I hit a home run—
By your words we gather

bringing you small stones
from County Cork in Ireland
your mother, father and brother found
in an April field of buttercups.

Tenderness

"A political act, let it be / tenderness."

—Leroi Jones

She placed a pillow between my legs—I was lying on my side—then another under my head. "Hug it," she said. Warmth. In a hospital room for medical procedures, on a long narrow table, about to receive an epidural for the pain in my lower back, I sensed the doctor coming, although I could not see him. At that moment, a second nurse facing me, the voice I didn't open my eyes to see, put his hand on my shoulder, his fingers rubbing round and round as the needle went in, the doctor quietly there. All of us together. Easing into the pillow I'd been given to hug, I gave myself to what lay ahead, an absence of pain, peace.

Living in the Line

When you read a poem,
each line beginning only to end
to begin again, don't run
ahead; pause to take in
what endings mean
and if you do
you'll feel the life
the words are lined up
to give you: letting go
giving birth   letting go

An Elegant Man   A Poet

A mentor was dying and I flew to be
At his side; a poem
I was writing, the rough draft
I recited to his wife, sensing him
Under the covers, listening,
His head lifting to the words.

What remains, the detail
Inside me, is how he,
As he was about to sneeze,
His wife offering Kleenex,
Took hold of the sheet
To blow into it the snot of himself
Bear he was—seeding the ground
On top of him.

2/2/22

The Apocalypse

Last night I saw the play,
Steven Sondheim's last,
Here We Are, Buñuel films
his inspiration: Act 1
sung by privileged folk
who want to be fed
with friends at their side
in a beautiful hotel:
"I could live here forever!"

Intermission. Time to stretch.

Act 2 and their music is gone!
Hands on the clock
stopped. No more food.
The actors are stuck!
While Sondheim was
working on this play, he died.
The apocalypse.
His play is the *here*
to live on.

V.

Thieving Beauty

"the distant past resounds"

—Gaston Bachelard

I lift a clause
from Gaston Bachelard,
convinced that it is good
to lift beauty
from under its cover
to keep it alive. Seeds grow
like semen when you make love
to make life. Words wait,
hidden and hungry
for breath, aiming to go forth
for generation. I open
a book by Jean Valentine
and lay it across the table
        Light me down to the long meadow
        to where the new snow falls on the fallen snow

Diaspora

The teapot whistles near a table set for
mother, father, two daughters, a family.
The suburbs. The year is 1969.

To the music of *Born Free*
our younger child dances on a stage.
She giggles over lemon pie
high with meringue. Yet under joy lies

duende, Spanish dance and Spanish men
she's driven toward (her history?
her destiny?). She will marry
an Argentinean from the mountains

whose father came from Spain. Familiar
with the night, comfortable on hidden paths,
he holds her through a buried life of exile.

Remember

in memory of Howard Ruskin
8/1931–1/2024

Reminded by the Rabbi we die twice
if we are not remembered, words
suddenly rise in me
from long ago—

When I was teaching *Hamlet,*
there it was—*Remember Me*—
the ghost of a father
urging his son "Remember me,"
which will in turn be Hamlet's
wish as he begs his good friend
to live to tell his story. His is tragic
but it lives as we witness Next.

Today my crossword-working,
polio-surviving brother-in-law, Howie,
lawyer, real estate man, "of infinite jest,"
determined (getting himself
kicked out of hospice) to be home
with his family, his martini, New Years Eve,
dies near his wife/my sister,
daughters and grandchildren,
leaving the dash of his life
to re-member.

found poems

I.

Three of us in the elevator:
a little girl, about five, in sunglasses,
her pretty mother in sleeveless cotton,
me, gray-haired, holding a cane, and
as I leave, the child turns to her mother,
"When I grow up, will you be old?"

II.

The night before my 92nd birthday
at the conference I've been going to
for over forty years, 10-year-old Bernard,
wise to plans for something special
cooked up for next day, tells me
"Good night and don't die."

To Wake in the World of
Sweetest Playgrounds

for Robert Bly and Tina Holt

I don't see dawn. I wake
        to these words turning into
I dosido, and I would like to
        wake to dance,
only my bladder
        is too full. I'll wet the sheets
and never mind dawn
or dance.

        All this is to say
                I am now free
to go to breakfast being served to
        the Great Mother
                and the New Father
calling out to the cook
        turning eggs into omelets
Make me one with everything

Called to Perform

I don't do mornings!
(my pajamas testify) and yet
to the court house I leap
this early morning

called to perform
jury duty. I must comply
in room 1121, watch two videos,
a rehearsal with men in ties

explaining what lies ahead
when/if I'm chosen. I lend an ear
but my eyes keep closing
so I say so

to the woman standing by
who asks my age—
92 in May I say—
flattered when she exclaims

g'wan! telling me I'm free
as she walks me to the exit—

if this were Broadway I'd be singing
Sondheim in the elevator

*Send in the clowns… there ought to be
clowns… maybe next year.*

VI.

A Wind Winding Up

It was the anniversary
of the *Communist Manifesto*—
it was being read
      on a barge
      on the Seine
      in Paris
and I was there with friends
for my birthday.

The wind kicked up—
      the pages fluttered
          and fell
              scattering—
the moderator bent to them

annoyed. "The wind,
      the patriarchal wind,"
she announced and reordered
      the ruffled pages.

We laughed and continued to
laugh each time the wind rose
      patriarchicly.
We were young, listening to history—

That day is history.
Conjuring "post-truth"
a showman blowing hot air
through loopholes is
President of the United States.

January 6th, 2021

Sitting in his white house
The Giant tweets
promising utopia—
     look look
at my great…

In a land without
a monarch he offers
celebrity, an entertainer
releasing energy one way
or another: a laugh, a lie, a fear—
you're fired—
   applause applause

In this month of transition
to the next president
the emperor refuses to leave.
Fired up, he shouts
     fight fight

and thousands rally
violently
to burn down our Capitol.

  *

I'd turned on TV
for celebration. In Georgia
a Jewish man and a black man
had been elected senators.

My mother used to cook a sweet and sour
tzimmis (Yiddish for "commotion")—

carrots, prunes sweet potatoes and
a marrow bone to usher in
the new year.
"Eat," she said, and we did.

She Wore a Wedding Dress of Glass

as the windows shattered
as the band was tuning up
as her vows were spoken

where once she was blessed
where her family was born
where all was to be broken

glass incised in every
garment   each word
each sentence spoken

no longer ordinary
star   concentration   oven
no longer to be innocent

in her city always trusted
with its windows of light
its Goethe and Mahler

poetry and arias
no more
without tears

after Anselm Kiefer's Die Schechina

56

The Bases of Peace

Last summer, leaving home
for Chestnut Hill, PA, Quaker-land,
I felt Peace. In a dream
Barack Obama, on base,
threw a ball across the field
to George Bush, as the world
sat in the stadium.

Years ago, my Dante teacher,
Bart Giamatti, who became
president of Yale, became
Commissioner of Baseball.
He believed in the art
of play, the divinity of
making one's way
home.

A Call to Arms

Today words come
through a cloud
across an ocean from
lands that refuse
to bury hatchets, where
arms murder, and
neighbors fear. *Arms*
become *arms* to bomb, shoot.

Underground, a friend
writes from a shelter;
she says help
everyone you know
to see both sides—
1000 Palestinian
and Israeli women
have formed Prayer of Mothers
to hold each other on Zoom.

Spears

In 1988 we flew home
from Africa. Masai men
had watched my husband
perform magic tricks
he'd learned from a friend.

In gratitude they gave him spears
we carried on the plane!
Hard to envision it today—
two spears up in the luggage rack!
Home they stand against our wall.

Domesticated, they've turned into
words: pears, then ears—
I hear my husband say
                    Presto!

VII.

18 Windows

My home has 18 windows
18 the number for life:
the sun comes in
to love me by day
and sends the moon
at night.

Pale yellow walls stay
in between the rounds
of *hello* and *goodbye*.
To enter take a lift
rising 12 floors
above the earth.

I heard my windows
swallow a letter
the year my husband
died. A widow I
remember the child
who always wanted to fly.

                    How
would you like to go up in the air,
up in the sky so blue?

I stare out 18 windows,
I dream in a bed for a king,
Dear Robert Louis Stevenson
let's build on the roof a swing.

Riding the Curl

Volute.
It's the curve
that speaks,
the pear
not the raspberry,
    an orange peel
                curled loose, hanging—
ivory sheath of a knife
opulent enough
     for paintings,
               Michelangelo's bridge
               over the Arno.
Song of a word
in the song of a city my city New York
where
       this hot afternoon
       air rolls from the rivers
            through my room
       from whatever heated lover
       rides its waves. *Volute*
           is all I need to say, ripe, cool
           volute,
to let its beauty
   take a turn with my body.

Breakfast

"When a bolt of lightning falls in love
with an old woman, sex is reinvented
as the world's first toaster oven"

—Laura Kasischke

A bagel lies in wait.

Open the oven door.
Slide it in.

The kettle sits steaming
on the stove.

Open the fridge
for the spread and

pull out the lox. Then
shmear it

on top of
the warm bagel.

Roof Garden

The gardener
said No
so I let it go

tending words:
hearing *tend*
as it grew

into *end—narrowing*
to *arrowing,* Eros
wooing me with loss.

Crossing the Street to Paradis

Crossing the street to *Paradis,*
A favorite café, sitting outside
With a blueberry scone, *The*
New York Times and a cappuccino
People pass, it's busy—
In front of me a tall man stops.
"Mom," he mutters so I look up
While his fingers unzip
To pull out and dangle his penis:

"How do you like my dick?"
He asks, and relaxed I answer
"I wasn't looking at it."
At that moment a young man
Behind me lurches forward and downs
The exhibitionist—socks him—
While the young woman with him
Keeps asking if I'm all right—
Yes I am, I say, I'm a New Yorker.

The tall man has run off.
My defenders, assured, walk on.
I return to *The Times* and
My cappuccino. A conversation
Walks by, something about
Hamlet and Central Park.
Are they talking about Joe Papp's
Shakespeare in the Park? Yes, they say,
And I say I love *Hamlet,* I taught it.

And I continue, "There's a Divinity
That shapes our ends, rough-hew them
How we will." He wants to know

My name. "Are you in it?"
I ask, and the slim man with the
Big smile says, "I'm Hamlet."

O What a Whirl

Astonishing! Going up
from down, the ground
no more the whole of it.
At one, then two years old—
pushing a self up up
O what a world!

I express it—
to Mama. She turns around.
Words give me entry,
saying *I do*, making family
up up! And now
switching direction: *up you go*
shrinking from view—lover
over   dearth to earth

       watching words
become an act
of striptease: strip
to trip, teasing,
easing me to
R I P

About the Author

Myra Shapiro, born in the Bronx, returned to New York City after forty-five years in Georgia and Tennessee where she married Harold Shapiro, raised two daughters and worked as a teacher and librarian. She holds a BA in American Literature (University of Chattanooga) MA in English (Bread Loaf School of English, Middlebury College) and MFA in Writing (Vermont College). She received the Dylan Thomas Poetry Award from The New School and was a finalist for the Robert H. Winner Award from the Poetry Society of America. She has held fellowships at the Banff Arts Center, MacDowell Colony, and Hedgebrook.

Shapiro's books of poetry are *I'll See You Thursday, 12 Floors Above the Earth, When the World Walks Toward You,* and her memoir, *Four Sublets: Becoming a Poet in New York.* Her poems have appeared in many periodicals and anthologies, and twice, in *Best American Poetry.* She serves on the Board of Directors of Poets House and teaches poetry workshops for the International Women's Writing Guild.

Acknowledgements

Special thanks to the editors of the following publications where these poems, some of which have been revised, first appeared.

I'll See You Thursday: "The Knowledge I Have Everything in the Garden"
Paterson Literary Review: "Locked-Down/Sweeping Up"
Ritualwell: "Passover 2020"
River Styx: "Put the Kettle On," (International Poetry Contest Winner, 2014)
The New Yorker: "These Are the Pearls"
When a Woman Tells the Truth: "Bastrop," "Put the Kettle On"
When the World Walks Toward You: "Put the Kettle On," "These Are the Pearls"
Write Forward: "A Call to Arms"

My deep gratitude to Carol Conroy, of blessed memory, who read the rough draft of this book; her words helped form it.

Thank you family and friends who helped my words become poems; thank you Ian Moran and Russell Hassell for your vision; Susan Weiman for your assistance; thank you Isla for your wisdom about pigeons. And thank you Chris Jansen and Norm Minnick for making this book happen.

A Note on the Type

Crossing the Street to Paradis
is set in Sabon,
designed by Jan Tschichold in 1964.
The Roman design is inspired
by the typefaces
of Claude Garamond (c. 1480–1561),
especially a specimen
printed by Konrad Berner,
a printer from Frankfurt.
Berner had married the widow
of printer Jacques Sabon,
after whom the typeface is named.
This elegant, highly readable typeface
is ideal for poetry.

www.ingramcontent.com/pod-product-compliance
Lightning Source LLC
Chambersburg PA
CBHW031247120626
46545CB00007B/2691